SUPERCHARGE

WORKFORCE

COMMUNICATION

To optimize digital transformation adoption, the workforce behind the technology solution needs to mastermind consciously connected communication.

— VALEH NAZEMOFF

SUPERCHARGE WORKFORCE COMMUNICATION

*6 Exercises that **Reshape Mindsets** to Optimize Digital Transformation Adoption*

VALEH NAZEMOFF

Bestselling Author of
The Four Intelligences of the Business Mind
and
The Dance of the Business Mind

TI Press

Supercharge Workforce Communication:
6 Exercises that Reshape Mindsets to Optimize Digital Transformation Adoption

This book is available at a discount when purchased in quantity for sales promotions or corporate use. Special editions, which include personalized covers, excerpts, and corporate imprints can be created when purchased in large quantities. For more information, please email media@acolyst.com or call 844.226.5978 ext. 106, or visit www.acolyst.com and www.valehnazemoff.com

First Edition
Paperback ISBN-13: 978-0-9987794-2-3

I dedicate this book to you, the reader, as you ignite the spark within to connect with all that matters.

Continually reshaping communication dynamics with compassionate intentions and emotions.

Embracing moments while experiencing the energy exchange journey that surrounds you!

People may hear your words, but they feel your attitude.

— JOHN C. MAXWELL

CONTENTS

Communication – the human connection – is the key to personal and career success.

—PAUL J. MEYER

CHAPTER 1 – ARE YOU CONNECTED?

Connection, the ability to feel connected, is neurobiologically wired, that's why we are here!
—Brené Brown

A FEW YEARS BACK, Walmart's IT Portfolio Strategy Manager approached me wanting communication techniques she could apply internally across their multicultural and multigenerational workforce. With over 11,000 retail stores, in more than 25 countries, and revenue of over $500 billion, Walmart employs more than 2 million people.

As I looked into her eyes, I could see the great concern she was facing. Language barriers wasn't her issue. She was disconnected from her team, the department and other departments within the organization. Maybe it was others disconnected from her. Either way, there was disconnection.

I fully understood and felt what she was going through. A year prior to meeting her, I went on a journey questioning what was happening in our business interactions with partners and clients. Executives I would engage with were all about measures and metrics. They would ask me what KPIs I would recommend for their specific environment and strategically what could be done to improve productivity and performance reporting. Something was missing. Something just didn't feel right.

I have been engaged with some of the most complex enterprise systems in the world involving big data and analytics and everything revolving around the data – infrastructure, security, applications, etc. Some of the questions I started asking, with a different lens were; *How do you know you have the right data to be analyzed? Are you making the best possible decision? Are you sure you collected everything? Could something be missing?*

Previously I would ask these questions, and many more, from a data only view. But then I started diving into the questions themselves, not the answer. I realized that many questions, such as the ones I posed above, trigger our emotions. It is our emotions that drive and affect our decisions.

It is the emotion of trust that gives us the confidence, or not, to believe in our answers. To believe in ourselves and believe in others we engage with. We need emotions to make impactful decisions. We need emotions to connect with others. It is when we are truly connected, that we can communicate in an engaged, enthused, and energetically supercharged way.

Emotions

Talking about emotions in the workplace is a touchy subject. Regardless, if it is your own emotion or of others. Most of my client and partner interactions are generally large enterprise organizations both in the private and public sectors. So, imagine the formality.

Let's, just you and I, let go of formality, and dive into the philosophical quest of *why emotion matters, especially in the workplace? And why connected emotions help us communicate and make better decisions?*

These decisions are not just leadership based. These decisions are when various teammates come together to finalize requirements for a new architectural or system design. Decisions on what the best competitive advantage is when assembling a solid team story. The collective decision for how to best handle a case or matter. Decisions are happening all the time. Face to face in meetings. Remotely via mobile device.

Further, these decisions are happening when human resources (HR) and internal marketing communications are not involved. Many associate internal communications and the contents and context surrounding it to be HR or marketing related. That is not the case. Absolutely not true. Communication is for all of us. Especially emotionally connected communication. No matter our role or position level in the organization. Each of us needs to be consciously aware for how we are communicating, emotionally, and the vibe we are sending and receiving. Yes, that is right. I did mean vibe.

Have you been in a meeting for a specific agenda, excited to share an idea or approach you had recently thought of and one person was just not engaged? They seemed distracted and preoccupied with something else? Where the vibe didn't feel that they were disinterested in what you had to say or in you, they just had something else on their mind?

I had that experience when I was engaged in a discussion with JPMorgan Chase Bank, N.A. (Chase Bank), a wholly-owned subsidiary of JPMorgan Chase & Co., global financial services firm with $2.5 trillion in assets and worldwide operations, about their digital transformation initiative. JPMorgan Chase & Co. made it publicly known that they were taking an "aggressive digital transformation" undertaking. They were already investing in research, innovation, and consumer feedback testing to determine many important factors such as, what matters most to millennials?

In their February 2018 Quarterly Report, they featured an entire dedicated section titled "Digital Everything" sharing with investors why digital mattered for their business. They addressed consumer mindsets and decisions of millennials leaving for a better competitive technology platform in addition to a lack of integrated digital communication channel. The resolution to attracting, engaging and enhancing the customer experience was by making the application accessibly convenient, friendly, secure, integrated and cost effective.

Yet Chase Bank was preoccupied with something else on their mind.

As I eagerly awaited to share and brainstorm various, creative, neuro-psychology based techniques to changing customer behavior and thought leading strategic ideas for digital adoption, the conversation was redirected. There was a pressing issue that took priority and needed attention and resolution. Internal communication.

One of the objectives for Chase Bank's digital transformation initiative has been to increase the slow consumer's use of their digital wallet, called Chase Pay. Chase Pay digital wallet project is highly visible as millions of dollars of investment has been made and anticipation for successful growth has been announced by executive leaders. Chase Bank is not the only one with a drive to increase consumer digital wallet transaction; Apple Pay, Google Pay, Samsung Pay, Walmart Pay, and PayPal are among products being invested for innovative researched techniques in figuring out ways to attract and exceed user experience expectation resulting in optimal adopted use.

But Chase Bank knows that to be positioned as the undisputed leader in digital financial services and payments, and stick to their mission statement, "to enable delivery of highly personalized, real-time experiences that customers increasingly expect," they need to tackle and address internal communication concerns first, as a high priority.

I had to set the meeting agenda aside and redirect my focus from user experience and adoption to supercharging workforce communication with de-centralized teams. The good news was that Chase Bank was aware of the internal disconnect needing to be addressed.

Philosophical Quest

Going back to our philosophical quest of *why emotion matters, especially in the workplace? And why connected emotions help us communicate and make better decisions?* – if we observe closely and objectively, we notice that when the workforce is connected, emotionally, a bond is formed. A bond of trust. That trust enhances productivity and performance. It creates loyalty, a meaningful purpose in the work environment. A culture of resilient togetherness to accomplish great achievements.

You need this trusting bond to come together to drive the company forward and be positioned competitively. The trusting bond allows engaged brainstorming sessions to happen, positive challenging ideas to appear, and meaningful actions to blossom.

Transforming workforce communication, impacts personal lives, community, society, politics and the world. We can each do our part in enhancing internal communication with the consciousness that it does create a ripple effect impact – let's make sure, together, it leads toward positive change!

Connected Society

As a society it is amazing how digitally connected we have become. The advancement of technology has made my own personal life much easier. I can spend more quality time with my family, able to process errands digitally, and transact purchases so I can shift my attention to more important matters and doing more of the things I love; dancing, traveling, writing, the list goes on.

Yet as a society, it is sad how we are humanly disconnected. Human connection is not about being connected through social media and counting the number of followers you now have and how many are viewing or liking your stories. It is about being more empathetic and compassionate towards each other.

Billionaire Jeff Hoffman, co-founder of Priceline (now part of Booking Holdings with a market cap value of $100 billion post acquisition of Booking.com), watched me shed tears as he shared how he and the other founding executives made a conscious collective decision to shift the mindset of the company from just selling airline tickets to being a compassionately mindful purpose driven company for how they were serving others; getting people to monumental events at an affordable price.

Jeff continued with his stories. Stories of his humanitarian activities. Stories of how he travels continent to continent working with various schools, students, small businesses, entrepreneurs. Stories how he still innovates and solves big problems – for example, the self-check-in kiosks that you now commonly see at airports, the ones that prints your boarding passes after you scan or insert information, is thanks to him. But I was shedding tears for the compassionate workplace stories he was sharing – where he built an environment, a culture, of learning what his employee's personal goals were, what they were aiming for, and really helping them achieve it. One example he shared was of an employee whose father, a police officer, died in the line of duty. The young man's goal was to buy a home for his mother and be able to care for her. Jeff helped the man grow professionally and supported him in achieving his personal goals.

Jeff is an example of being authentically and compassionately connected to those in the workplace and surrounding encounters. As he continued with many more stories that touched my soul, something sparked within me. An energetic shift; an awakening. It was that moment I made a conscious decision. I needed to do my part in society by reshaping mindsets to supercharge workforce communication.

Digital Transformation

Robotic Process Automation (RPA), Artificial Intelligence (AI), Machine Learning (ML), Deep Learning (DL) and other digital technology are designed to enhance and ease our current activities, manage workload, and free us from unnecessary mundane repetitive tasks. They are to help us with big data analytics; recognizing patterns, taking actions, and altering learned behaviors to do more within the boundaries it has been programmed to do.

Going back towards the beginning of this chapter, being curious about the types of questions we are asking about the data: *How do you know you have the right data to be analyzed? Are you making the best possible decision? Are you sure you collected everything? Could something be missing?* We know that at some point in time the data was human driven; programmed with certain calculations and criteria to be captured and processed.

If we look at the GPS and the purpose it now serves, it is to help remove the task of us humans trying to determine best route for faster arrival time; instead giving us the freedom to focus on other activities more important – sharing stories with my mother on our drive out of town.

Because of this freedom to alter the state of mind, humans will be able to transform to higher level thinking and involvement of initiatives. Researching, designing and testing for new, improved ways to exceed user experience and enhance adoption. Crafting methods to outshine the competition. Discussing best course of action for open cases and matters. In other words, coming together in a collective collaborative manner, with enthusiasm and energy, delivering additional value and service to internal and external customers.

Intention of This Book

After several years of interacting in challenging and dramatically dynamic environments with various personalities, cultures, and generational experiences, this book teaches you to be consciously aware of communication exchange that become part of the subconscious and provide breakthrough moments (Chapter 2). My goal is to inspire you, through my own recent experiences, and one of my client's, with practical actions and insights, not theory, in reshaping mindsets to building a cohesive, collaborative, and trusting environment (Chapter 3). I will explain about Transformational Intelligence and how it can impact and optimize digital transformation adoption (Chapter 4). Further, I am excited to share a story of a communication engagement technique, you can put into practice, that I applied at one of the White House, Executive Office of the President's agency components; Office of the United States Trade Representative (Chapter 5) and many more "aha" moments to help you thrive.

First Exercise

Before we dive in to the next chapter, I have an exercise for you. Here are the steps:

1. Identify someone you work with who you <u>feel</u> appears distracted and preoccupied. Someone who you <u>feel</u> is not focused on the priority of the day. The goal here is to take the time to see how you can help someone else with a situation that doesn't involve getting you ahead in your own agenda, your own task or priority. This is to truly selflessly be there for someone else.

2. Take a few deep breaths in and out. Set an intention that you want to genuinely help the person you identified. Create a timeframe in your mind – for example, dedicating 30 minutes of undistracted quality time so it does not take away from your own daily priorities.

3. With a warm welcoming smile, approach the person you identified. Share that you <u>felt</u> they might be distracted, need help with something, or just need to talk to a work friend. Then let them know

that you have 30 minutes (or however much time you set in your mind) of undistracted time to give.

4. If they do share with you what they do need help with, great. If they need more of your time, then honestly and respectfully communicate if adjustments can be made or not. If they are not willing to share and you felt brushed off, that is completely okay! Just say you can be there for them if needed in the future and when they are ready. Then walk away.

If you work remotely, or in a de-centralized team environment, you could do the same over the phone and/or through digitally connected devices. That's the beauty of technology. You can sense, or get a vibe, when someone is distracted and doesn't seem their usual self by paying attention to how patterns of their behavior have altered. Offer to be there for them using the steps above.

Now, I genuinely want to hear from you. And as this chapter title asks, *Are You Connected?* I am curious to know how this first exercise worked out for you. You don't have to provide me all the details, but in general what you felt, how you approached, and what the outcome was – what shifts you noticed. Please connect with me on this landing page: www.acolyst.com/communication

There will be a form. Once you fill out and submit, I will personally be notified. This form will help me determine what exercise and stage of the book process you are at. When it comes to communication there are so many elements and factors to consider. I am here for you because I want this to be a success. I am excited for your journey ahead. Looking forward to connecting with you!

Every exercise step I share with you in this book is important and will be useful to you. It is an opportunity for you to observe and learn more about yourself and your colleagues at work. You will then be able to decide what works for you, what you want to change, and then begin to see how the human transformation evolves. It is important to remember to be patient. A seed does not blossom into a flower overnight.

See you in the next chapter to learn more about conscious awareness, where together, it leads us to transform and supercharge workforce communication.

CHAPTER 2 – CONSCIOUSLY CONNECTED COMMUNICATION

*Effective communication is 20% what you know
and 80% how you feel about what you know.*
—Jim Rohn

SUMMER OF 2015, I had travelled to the Windy City presenting to entrepreneurs and executives who were in the business of making impacts by providing technology solutions; products and services. The room filled event was hosted by CompTIA, a non-profit IT focused trade association, headquartered in Illinois, that educates on various technology related subjects and provides professional technical certifications, internationally. More than 2 million professionals have received a certification since the organization was established in 1982. CompTIA has also made significant impacts with their philanthropy and advocacy practice for more than 50 million industry professionals surrounding the $5 trillion global IT ecosystem.

That year, CompTIA's yearly event, ChannelCon, was held near the Chicago River. Their theme was *Minds in Motion*. Sticking to the theme, my presentation was titled, "Transform from the Inside Out: Building Internal Effectiveness while Growing Your Business."

As I presented, I asked the attendees how they would define *efficiency* versus *effectiveness*. At first, some used the words interchangeably. Then when we went through the definitions and they started to really put their minds in motion, efficiency was classified as reducing costs and re-evaluating resources. Efficiency is looking at what you already have and thinking of ways to improve and maximize what already exists, aiming to do more with less, even replace.

Effectiveness on the other hand is more emotional. It requires a different altered state of mind; of impactful creativity, innovation and growth. Effectiveness requires new ways of communication and collaboration. It is about understanding the psychology of human behaviour to create new, positive workforce habits.

The mindset of effectiveness should not be to maximize efficiency. The mindset is to create new - new jobs, connections, products, services, applications, markets, acquisitions, etc. To be forward thinking. The effectiveness mindset is often used to be strategically competitive; but that is not always the case.

Figure 2-1. Efficiency versus Effectiveness Mindset

Balancing Mindset

Within my presentation, I used Google's driverless car (self-driving) program as an example. Being forward thinking, Google was effective in their mindset to invest and be innovative with their driverless car program. Unfortunately, during testing an incident occurred. An incident that was not Google's driverless fault. Another car, with a human driver, who was texting, hit the self-driving car. The incident that occurred caused an evaluation to be done back at Google. The evaluation meant that the team at Google needed to circle back and be efficient and effective at the same time. Fixing what already existed and coming up with something new that they did not calculate and account for.

To be effective, you need to be forward thinking and making an impact. It doesn't have to be disruptive or innovative. It just needs to be impactful. This applies to the various roles in an organization.

Looking at the business development and sales roles, there is a difference between efficient and effective way of thinking and balancing both. An example of efficiency could be cross selling and upselling to existing accounts. An example of effectiveness could be thinking of impactful ways to sell into new accounts and bringing in what is now referred to as "new logos" for the business. The impactful ways could be innovative, disruptive, or not. You could take what already worked in the past and give it a creative approach for attracting new business. For a new account, new logo, new target, new market, you need a starting point. That starting point causes a different state of mind, a state of creativity and possibilities. Thinking of what worked in the past and applying it to the new, thinking of new innovative methods of approach, or being completely disruptive by partnering with someone you typically would not partner with but do because it gives you a strategic competitive angle.

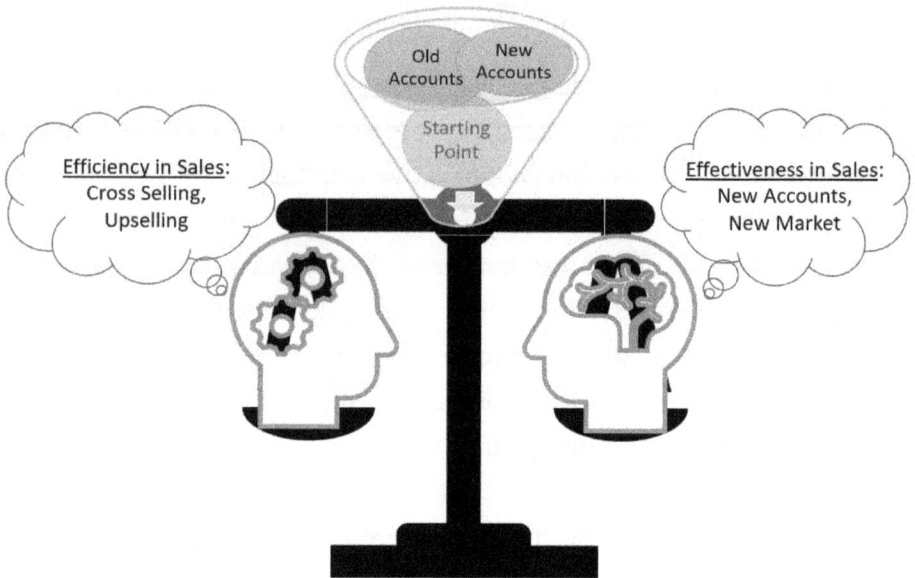

Figure 2-2. Balancing Mindset in Sales Role (Within Same Person)

Second Exercise

You are already aware of the difference between efficiency and effectiveness, I know. But what is key here, and what I assure will make a huge impact is balancing. Being able to bounce your mind back and forth between the two. When training the mind to consciously become mindful of thinking between efficiency versus effectiveness, you not only become more focused and organized, but the communication within the organization dramatically improves, if others are practicing these methods as well. But it needs to start with you. Each one of us is responsible for doing our part and taking the step. The biggest first step to this portion of the exercise is putting it into writing. Why? Because you need to do the following exercise for it to work. Here are the steps:

1. Take a sheet of paper and split into two columns; efficiency and effectiveness

(Note: visit this link www.acolyst.com/communication to download the template for this exercise)

2. List the activities or tasks you are working on right now. Putting each into either the efficiency or the effectiveness column, not in both.

3. Then for each column, order them in priority. Numbering next to each activity under each column what you believe takes more precedence than the other tasks.

Balancing Multi-Role Focus

The same is true for a focused group within an organization with multiple roles. Let's look at the content team. Sometimes they are part of the marketing group, other times part of the technical, product or research and development group. Other times content is a division of their own, supporting other departments like HR, compliance, etc. Within the content team there could be designated roles such as a content manager and a content strategist.

Typically, the content manager focuses on efficient activities. Taking existing materials and improving them to draw purposeful attention to the audience they are targeting. For example, imagine the product development team needs new security requirement announcements to be shared with existing customers. The development team syncs with the content manager to give existing materials from development that now need to be repurposed to distribute as external announcements.

Another example would be HR needing to make sure proper announcements about their wellness program is being properly distributed internally to employees. The focus for the content manager is to update materials, by converting text information to visual, using infographics.

On the other hand, a content strategist could possibly focus more on effective matters. Such activities could include focusing on attracting new clientele, new logos, new brands, and new partnerships. Often content strategists would work with marketing teams in supporting demand and lead capture activities; defining and addressing best content route for higher conversion rate.

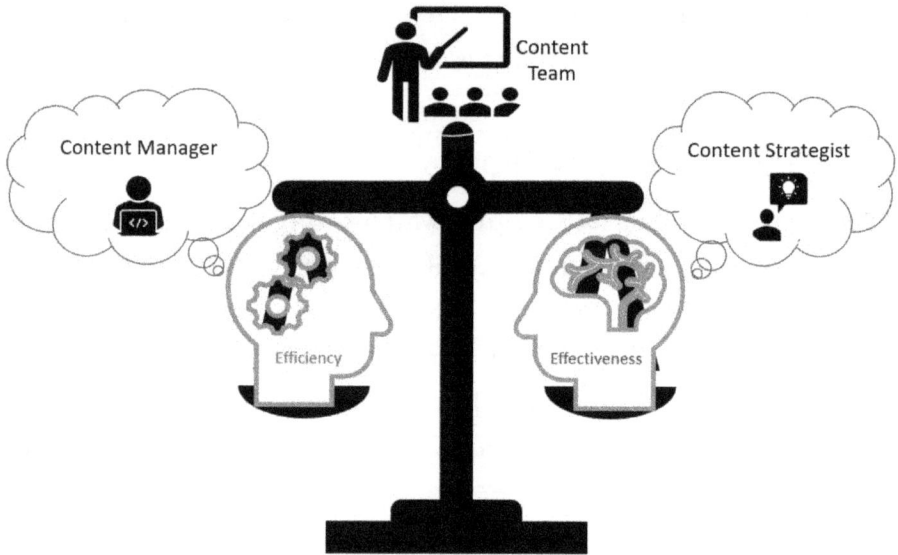

Figure 2-3. Balancing Mindsets Between 2 Roles (Within Same Group)

Third Exercise

Now that you have your list broken out into two different columns, efficiency versus effectiveness, and have numbered it sequentially according to your thoughts on priority, <u>without sharing your list</u>, have other members on your team or group that might have the same or similar role as you, and even slightly different, go through the Second Exercise. Once they are finished, have a team meeting to compare. Here are the steps for that meeting:

1. Once your colleague, teammate, or group have come together, prior to sharing and exchanging each other's list, agree that this is an exercise to help each other become better united, connected and collaborative. Agree that your meeting space is a nonjudgmental zone and stay open minded. If having a mediator or liaison makes you and your teammates feel more comfortable to get you started, then have one.

    > *Note: Ways to create an environment where participants are engaging freely, welcoming ideas and discussions, is shared in my first book, The Four Intelligences of the Business Mind: How to Rewire Your Brain and Your Business for Success, in Chapter 5, titled "Mastermind Intelligence." You can find more information by visiting this link* www.acolyst.com/communication

2. Now share each other's list or use some examples from different individual list. The intent is to compare for discussion purposes. There is no right or wrong answer. Just difference in perception and perspective.

3. Notice the differences among the individuals. Pay attention to the different priorities set. Observe, without judgment, what was classified as efficiency versus effectiveness. Even if someone on the team does not have the exact role as you, still observe what their perspective is. Perceive what they assume the team's priority should be and what they have categorized as efficient versus effective.

4. Then have an open-minded discussion to learn about each other's perspective. Why each listed the tasks on the columns and prioritized the way they did.

5. Discuss how different it is? Does everyone have the exact same understanding for what the priority should be? Is everyone viewing the difference between efficiency versus effectiveness? Do definitions need to be revisited? What could the team do to be more

efficient and more effective? There is no right or wrong industry set answer. This needs to be tailored specific to your environment; to your group. The goal is to be curious to improve communication exchange.

This exercise is meant with the intention of creating awareness. To bring open dialogue and discussion where everyone involved can participate in. It is for you to be consciously aware of how connected, or disconnected, you are with your colleagues, team, and group. And mindful of the true engagement that exists within the team members. This exercise is not meant to judge anyone. It is simply to learn from each other and be conscious of each other's perspective. Everyone has a different experience, background and understanding. The key is to work together to help each other come to an agreement on a new one so you can collectively thrive on the organization's goals, objectives and initiatives. This awareness exercise is one of many that helps supercharge workforce communication.

Balancing Organizational Priorities

The priority for efficiency and effectiveness could also come from a division or department within the organization that sets the balanced standards for the rest of the organization. For example, the compliance department and analyst teams supporting compliance related functions could split the efficient versus effective activities among the division members. Some compliance analysts could focus on efficient activities by making sure the organization is following guidelines set by regulators. They could do this through training, distributed announcements, or some type of review and check-in information capture. At the same time other compliance analysts in the department could focus on effective type of activities, such as addressing new ways to train personnel, like with cartoon images. Others would provide updates for new information being regulated, such as when General Data Protection Regulation (GDPR) was a mandate for data privacy with a crunch deadline to be implemented. This type of compliance focus would also require teaming with other departments within the organization, such as security, finance, IT, HR, sales, marketing, operations, and others.

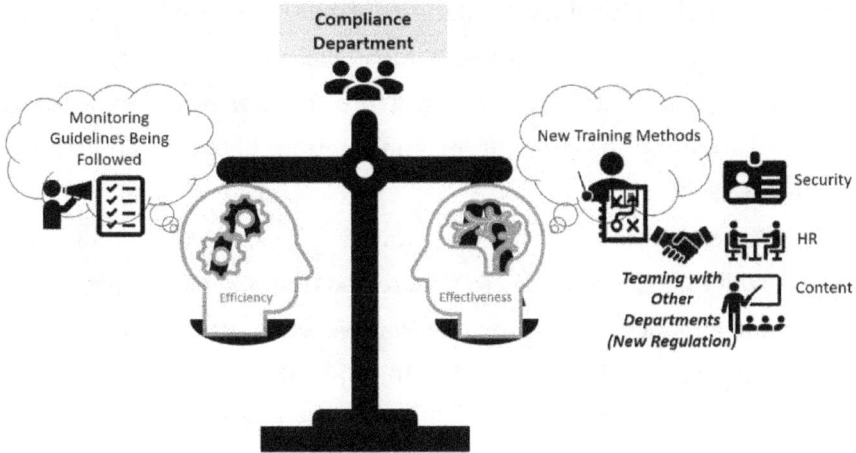

Figure 2-4. Balancing Mindsets Within a Department or Division

On-Going Spin Looped Cycle

Now that you can see how the balance of efficiency and effectiveness can be applied to individual roles, teams, divisions, departments and the organization, let's drill in and focus on just the efficiency portion for a moment.

Going back to Google's driverless program referenced at the beginning of this chapter, we find when they evaluated the incident post the car accident, there was a need to enhance and improve (efficiency) the program and - in parallel or coinciding manner - apply new requirements (effectiveness), not previously accounted for.

Same for any program. When we evaluate, consistently, and focus on efficiency, often the need to adjust and be impactful arises and that is when your mindset shifts to one of effectiveness.

It is a spin looped cycle. Within the cycle of efficiency thinking, an effective thinking seed is sparked and then it starts to blossom on a trail of its own, while the efficiency thinking continues. Then when the effective thinking is now in effect, and needs to be maintained, it then loops back again into efficiency mode of thinking. The mind is then constantly moving in cycles, jumping in and out of the motion between efficiency and effectiveness.

When my own company, Acolyst, wanted to be efficient by reducing cost to invest back into the company to update and upgrade technology, knowing we needed to enhance and improve the way we were doing business, we came to terms and agreed that we needed to apply the new; transitioning and moving to the cloud. Moving to the cloud for us was being effective. It was impactful for our business. It wasn't a disruptive concept or an innovative one, but an impactful one. Again, being effective can be disruptive or it can be innovative, but it doesn't have to be. It just needs to be impactful.

Cycle of Creativity and Breakthrough Moments

There is a critical reason why I continually emphasize the importance of effectiveness being impactful yet not always innovative or disruptive.

It has to do with the ability to balance stress. Stress can be a good thing, helping our bodies and brains stay sharp and alert. Like when taking a test or writing a book. However, when highly stressed, due to fear (missing deadlines, losing job, contract, business, etc.), it tends to be the enemy of creativity and kills it. Not always though.

Studies have shown that lower stressed environments do tend to lead to higher levels of creative thinking. Thus, many companies (Google, Microsoft, Facebook, Amazon, Apple, etc.) started redesigning their workplaces to spark ideas by making it more colorful and playful.

Further, when the worry is less on competition and loss, the mindset can re-focus more on vision, creativity and innovation. For example, when Apple's Steve Jobs stopped focusing his mind on ways to compete with Microsoft, after losing sales from $11 billion in 1995 to $7 billion in 1997, he was then able to take the reins and re-build the company to one of the top brands in the world. One of the many techniques that fueled him for the innovative breakthrough experienced was Jobs knowing he had cheering user audiences on the sidelines - the 20 to 25 million devoted users who believed and supported Macintosh.

I've asked my champion dance friends what fuels them with energy under the stress of competing to keep going, remaining positive, and carrying on movements that sometimes require improvisation. The energy comes from spectators cheering them on, where they redirect their focus to inspiring the audience through their dance movements. Beating their competition is secondary focus. Primary is the core purpose for the passion behind why they started dancing to begin with.

You don't have to consistently think of innovating and disrupting like Steve Jobs to be successful at making impacts. Success comes in many varieties. You can impact through an outstanding customer service and/or partner program.

Focus on the initial layer of figuring out a solution that would impact. And if the solution happens to be innovative or disruptive, consider that a bonus! When your mind has let go of the fear and worry, that is when creativities and breakthroughs happen.

For more insight information to the science of breakthrough moments, exercises for refocusing the mind from worrying to creating, and balancing stress, make sure to visit my website landing page for more information - www.acolyst.com/communication

Workforce Behind the Technology

Now, I want to dive into the relation of what you have learned so far with efficiency and effectiveness and how it plays a part on your path to optimizing digital transformation adoption or any other transformational initiatives that your organization is focusing on. Recall, the focus of this chapter is to teach you to be consciously aware of communication exchange that become part of the subconscious and provide breakthrough moments.

Starting with some basic definitions, digital transformation is about using technology to enhance and impact the user experience. The user can be internal or external. Adoption, specifically digital adoption, is meant for the user to use the technology to its fullest capability for the intended purposes of the solution.

> *To optimize digital transformation adoption, the workforce behind the technology solution needs to mastermind consciously connected communication.*

How? First, focus on understanding who the workforce is behind the technology solution. Then, determine how to mastermind consciously connected communication. There are two workforce categories to consider:

1. The end users of the technology
2. The solution drivers of the technology

| The workforce designing, building, supporting the digital technology [Inclusive of product vendor, services consulting firm, and customers driving the project] | The workforce using the digital technology (internal / external users) [Addressing workforce of the future; multi-generational & multi-cultural gap] |

Figure 2-5. Two Workforce Categories for Digital Technology

An ideal scenario of the solution driving workforce team would be the collective minds of the product vendor, services consulting firm and the various customer stakeholder, decision makers and end user champion leads, sometimes referred to as the super users, to work in unison. Product vendors focusing on the "out-of-the-box" features and benefits with the services consulting professionals focusing on the solutions to be tailored or customized based on the customer required needs. Crafting, driving and delivering the best technology solution, based on the researched psychology behavior of the end user, requires harmonious synergy as a united workforce.

This unison occurs when all three parties have effectively masterminded consciously connected communication. You do this by focusing on the Three E Model™, which is inclusive of three focus groups:

- Internal Efficiency
- Internal Effectiveness
- External Effectiveness

Three E Model™

Picture a sales team within an organization where a workforce team has now completed the design and build of a digital transformation solution. For sales to drive revenue, bring additional business, and keep customers engaged and loyal, they need some form of internal support. That internal support would be split into efficient and effective activities. Internal efficient support could be those maintaining existing customer relationships, such as the customer relationship manager roles (aka customer success teams). Internal effective support could be the proposal team. Focusing on what partners to draw in, what existing resources could be key for making an impact to new opportunities, and what other ways to leverage to win. The external effective support could be marketing driving leads through various activities such as event engagement, blogging, and partnership outreach programs.

All three focus groups, Three E Model™, are necessary for sales to focus on driving revenue.

Another area within an organization focusing on transformation initiatives could be the Three E Model™ split into client solutions. Using my company, Acolyst, as an example, here is how I've mapped the Three E Model™ to solution sets:

1. Internal Efficiency = Operational Cooperation
2. Internal Effectiveness = Business Collaboration
3. External Effectiveness = Strategic Coordination

Specific client project examples I headed, mapping to the Three E Model™ are:

1. Operational Cooperation for the United States Postal Service (USPS) CIO Office, an agency that delivers about 485 million pieces of mail every day, employs more than 7.5 million people, and generates approximately $70 billion in revenue. The CIO Office needed a strategy of **internal efficiency** to communicate the value of IT to other internal executive departments (CFO, CMO, COO), demonstrating improvements with responsiveness, cost, resources, technology and more.

2. Business Collaboration for the Pension Benefit Guaranty Corporation (PBGC), an agency that protects retirement security and incomes of nearly 40 million Americans. The organization's steering committee required **internal effectiveness** for an integrated solution to address performance gaps due to years of uncoordinated management, separate and disconnected systems, and duplicative and inconsistent information, between two of the four units within PBGC's Office of

Negotiations & Restructuring (ONR), formerly Insurance Program Office (IPO):

- Corporate Finance and Restructuring Department (CFRD), formerly the Department of Insurance Supervision and Compliance (DISC), and
- Office of Chief Counsel (OCC)

3. Strategic Coordination for the White House, Executive Office of the President (EOP). One of the tasks EOP wanted, was a strategy of **external effectiveness** for adoption of an enterprise-wide solution across the 10 EOP components:

The White House Office; Office of the Vice President; Office of Administration; Office of Management and Budget; Office of the United States Trade Representative; Office of National Drug Control Policy; Counsel of Economic Advisors; Counsel on Environmental Quality; National Security Council; and the Office of Science and Technology Policy.

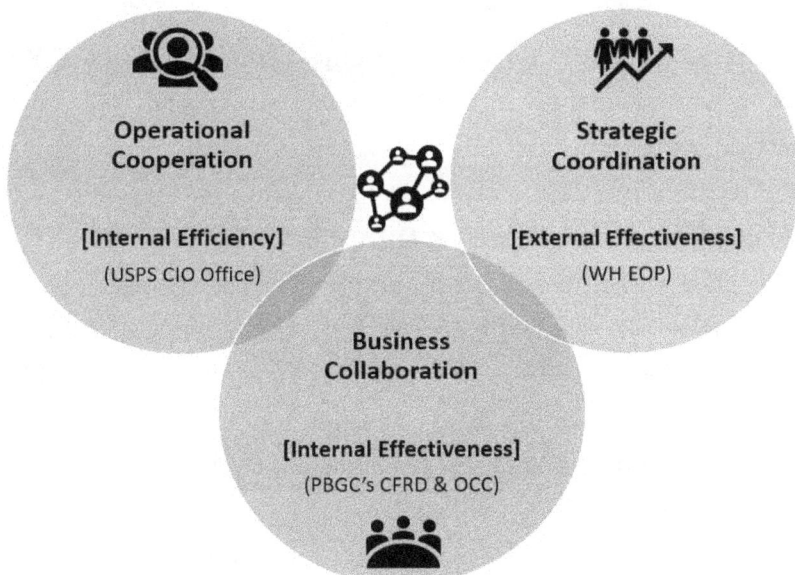

Operational Cooperation

[Internal Efficiency]
(USPS CIO Office)

Strategic Coordination

[External Effectiveness]
(WH EOP)

Business Collaboration

[Internal Effectiveness]
(PBGC's CFRD & OCC)

Figure 2-6. Client Project Examples Using the Three E Model™

Solution Set Thinking

For Acolyst, Operational Cooperation is essential when a group of people need to thrive and carry forward a joint message in a streamlined manner. Operational Cooperation is monitoring the operation and understanding how to find ways to complement opposing thoughts and behaviors to be **internally efficient**: a bidirectional relationship that exchanges information, performance, and action.

Business Collaboration is about increasing productivity and inviting a healthy give and take between partners and parties involved. Collaboration is longer term than cooperation. There are more dynamics involved to be **internally effective**.

Strategic Coordination is about moving different elements harmoniously together for **external effectiveness**.

Three E Model™ in Partnership

Not necessarily do the three focus groups within the Three E Model™ need to be within one organization mapped to solution sets based on corporate capability.

Three separate companies can come together, in partnership, to drive a market initiative forward. I am a big fan and huge supporter of partnership, especially when the cultural mindset, purpose, and intention are consciously connected, as is the case with Acolyst and two of our partners, Federal Resources Corporation (FRC) and Vector Resources, Inc (VRI). I will share with you how our partnership is formed using the Three E Model™, so you can also identify complementary focus areas with your partners that make sense for your business.

With digital transformation consistently evolving, so is the strategy around interconnected initiatives such as cybersecurity. Focusing on the Three E Model™, we looked at the current demanding changes related to digital technology and needs around cybersecurity against each partner's strengths. Three of the main digital changes impacting cybersecurity are:

1. External Attacks
2. Business Needs
3. Digital Technology Architecture

FRC's strength is in Operational Cooperation; maintaining, monitoring and managing for **internal efficiency** matters. Thus, FRC's focus in relation to our partnership around cybersecurity is defending against external attacks by improving and upgrading the technology that already exists. Acolyst's strength is in Business Collaboration; addressing compliance, risk assessments, audits, and communication strategy plan for **internal effectiveness**. Hence, re-examining business models, processes and focusing on the business needs to adopt new workforce approaches and cultural change. VRI's strength is in Strategic Coordination; working alongside partners, customers, and stakeholders, to streamline DevOps activities that need constant feedback to roll out new changes for **external effectiveness**. Therefore, in relation to cybersecurity, making impactful improvement in productivity, time to deliver, and rapid development that enables faster and stronger protection measures and response.

Figure 2-7. Three E Model™ in Partnership

Three E Model™ for Service Level Agreements (SLAs)

The Three E Model™ can also be used when establishing service expectations and delivery agreements. Figure 2-8 provides an example where the Three E Model™ is used to break out the different types of Service Level Agreements (SLAs): internal, supplier, and customer.

Figure 2-8. Three E Model™ for Service Level Agreements (SLAs)

Mastermind Consciously Connected Communication

Now that you have a variety of examples of how I've applied the Three E Model™, it is your turn to make a conscious effort in mapping it out for yourself based on your organization's initiatives. By applying and practicing, you become more aware of the communication exchange that occurs. Over time it becomes part of your subconscious, as it is part of mine, making it a habit to look at opportunities in a Three E Model™ way.

Be mindful that maintaining an enthusiastically curious attitude towards discovery of efficient and effective solution is one powerful way that will lead you to breakthrough moments. This will help with awareness for the need in reshaping mindsets to building a cohesive, collaborative, and trusting environment, which is our focus in the next chapter.

CHAPTER 3 – AWARENESS IN RESHAPING COMMUNICATION

Awareness is conscious connection with universal intelligence. Another word for it is Presence: consciousness without thought.
—*Eckhart Tolle*

THE U.S. CONGRESS has an investigative arm called the Government Accountability Office (GAO). It is an independent, nonpartisan agency that supports Congress in meeting constitutional responsibilities. Additionally, GAO's other initiative includes improving the performance of the federal government and ensuring accountability to Americans.

One action GAO takes is publishing standards and principles for federal agencies to follow. Often, state, local, quasi-governmental entities, not-for-profit organizations, have the option of adopting these frameworks. Private sectors can also utilize them as best practice framework guides.

Two notable standards and principles the GAO has published involving workforce communication are:

- Human Capital: Key Principles for Effective Strategic Workforce Planning (GAO-04-39; 2003)
- Standards for Internal Control in the Federal Government (GAO-14-704G; 2014)

Notice that one document is from 2003 and the other published in 2014. For more than a decade then, and still today, the GAO has been consistently reporting on workforce communication related needs. The Human Capital (2003) document emphasizes that success comes by aligning workforce planning to the mission and programmatic goals of the organization via collaboration, inclusion, and sharing. For example:

"[GAO has] found that efforts that address key organizational issues, like strategic workforce planning, are most likely to succeed if, at their outset, agencies' top program and human capital leaders set the overall direction, pace, tone, and goals of the effort, and involve employees and other stakeholders in establishing a communication strategy that creates shared expectations for the outcome of the process."

However, the Internal Control (2014) document accentuates management controlling the communication throughout the process by which the entity tries to achieve its objective: "management should," "management communicates," "management receives," etc. Further, GAO defines information system to be:

"An information system is the people, processes, data, and technology that management organizes to obtain, communicate, or dispose of information."

See following Table 3-1 differentiating the two document mindsets.

Table 3-1. GAO Human Capital vs. Internal Control Document Communication Differences

Human Capital: Key Principles for Effective Strategic Workforce Planning (2003)
Involving top management, _employees_, and other stakeholders in developing, communicating, and implementing the strategic workforce plan.
Consider opportunities for **reshaping** the workforce by reengineering current work processes, **sharing** work among offices within the agency and with other agencies that have similar missions.

Standards for Internal Control in the Federal Government (2014)
Management should **internally** communicate the necessary quality information to achieve the entity's objectives: • Management communicates quality information throughout the entity using established reporting lines. • Management communicates quality information down and across reporting lines to enable personnel to perform key roles in achieving objectives, addressing risks, and supporting the internal control system. • Management receives quality information about the entity's operational processes that flows up the reporting lines from personnel to help management achieve the entity's objectives. • Management selects appropriate methods to communicate internally.
Management should **externally** communicate the necessary quality information to achieve the entity's objectives: • Management communicates with, and obtains quality information from, external parties using established reporting lines. • Management communicates quality information externally through reporting lines so that external parties can help the entity achieve its objectives and address related risks. • Management receives information through reporting lines from external parties. • Management selects appropriate methods to communicate externally.

When one mindset is inclusive - which is generally what happens with HR departments - yet another mindset is directive and controlling; thus, the name of the document, Internal Control – which is generally what happens between lines of business and IT management - a disinterest and lack of effort occurs within the culture of the organization when adopting systems and technology post implementation. Why? Because employees don't feel responsible, it is management's responsibility. How do I know? Experience.

Behavioral Traits

Back in 2008, my company, Acolyst, was the prime contractor for PBGC's Early Warning Program (EWP) Risk Management Early Warning (RMEW) system. PBGC having over $112 billion in assets, considers this program and system highly profiled and visible; focusing on corporate transactions involving companies with financial troubles and considerably underfunded pension plans. PBGC's mission is to protect America's retirement security and pays pension benefits when companies cannot.

I was the executive project manager leading the digital transformation effort of collaborating and updating communication flow by streamlining and automating business workflow processes of two internal departments; financial and legal. The goal was to coordinate and connect systems, information, and manage workload. Additionally, the project scope included modernizing the application and retiring two legacy systems while migrating, integrating and reporting on the data and documents. Integration with seven other systems was also necessary.

Having a psychology background with a focus and passion for organizational behavior, I insisted on a strategy for user adoption to be put into place for post go-live. However, what was approved by the client program manager for user adoption was a training plan with some computer-based training, guide manuals, and knowledge transfer.

Many assume that an adoption strategy only involves training, but that is not the case. There is more involved to making the digital technology adoption a success. Hint: it is not the technology itself. I had predicted, as a futurist and maybe as psychic, then, that there would be some difficulty in later years to come, based on the culture and style used by PBGC management. Back then the notion of user experience and the importance of system adoption was not common. Many assumed that implementing the latest modern technology would solve a lot of communication collaboration related issues. And even today, many still believe in that.

In 2009 the system launch was a success. I delivered the project on time and within budget. However, two years after I was gone, the Office of Inspector General (OIG) at PBGC initiated an internal audit review of the system lasting until 2014.

PBGC OIG auditors, observed some interesting behaviors for the system I implemented, RMEW, according to their report. Yet, what I want you to observe in Table 3-2 is the response given by the Chief of the Department, now called Office of Negotiations and Restructuring (ONR), under that program for two of the recommended changes.

Table 3-2. Chief of PBGC's Response for Two (2) of OIG's Recommendations

PBGC Assistant Inspector General for Audit; OIG **Recommendations**	**Chief** of Negotiations and Restructuring; ONR **Responses**
Train applicable staff in newly developed processes and RMEW required documentation and ensure periodic management review to ensure effectiveness of established internal controls.	... we believe this condition no longer exists. ... staff has been trained on the processes and procedures related to their roles and responsibilities in documenting, executing, monitoring, enforcing, and modifying.... Improvements to RMEW and the designation of a specific staff member ... have strengthened internal controls over these processes.
Ensure that RMEW procedures adequately incorporate federal guidance and PBGC policies and procedures for records management, so that staff consistently store, maintain and dispose of federal records.	...ONR staff is required to take annual records management training and has been trained in ONR requirements for uploading records to RMEW. Furthermore, ... a compliance review...is performed to ensure that all required documentation has been completed and uploaded into RMEW to ensure successful compliance monitoring.

The end users being trained within the ONR department are attorneys, paralegals, financial analysts and actuaries. PBGC's OIG recommended training and the Chief of PBGC's ONR department responded that training has been conducted and the "condition no longer exists" with a compliance review performed ensuring success.

When it comes to training staff on newly developed processes, training alone on the processes and procedures relating to their roles and responsibilities does not make the "condition" go away. Especially if it was a one-time training too. There will always be a condition for on-going improvement. How am I confident training on the processes and procedures relating to their roles and responsibilities was not enough? Because of cognitive psychology and what happens next.

In 2018, PBGC issued a request for proposal which included assistance to help the organization improve the program's communication efforts. Then January 2019, about 5 years post audit finding, where training was recommended, and about a decade after system go-live, we find out why. PBGC's OIG released a final evaluation report for the same program, EWP, after reviewing the Case Guidance and Monitoring Guidance documents, system, processes and procedures. The evaluation was triggered by plan sponsor complaints regarding the EWP program. PBGC's OIG specifically reviewed **external communication** information; company profile information, information request letter, case close out recommendations and case close out email. They also reviewed case details in the system for notes made by the analyst documenting the status of the case and their contact with the plan sponsor. The plan sponsors are the designated points of contact of the company or employer that sets up or administers the retirement plan; also known as company representatives.

The review was a formal process conducted under the authority of the Inspector General Act of 1978 and in accordance with the Quality Standards for Inspection and Evaluation issued by the Council of the Inspectors General on Integrity and Efficiency. Table 3-3 provides a list of findings per OIG's 2019 final evaluation report. The report was also delivered to the Board (inclusive of Department of Labor, Department of the Treasury, Department of Commerce) and Congress, for awareness of reducing risk and improving the efficiency and effectiveness of PBGC EWP program and operation.

Table 3-3. PBGC OIG's 2019 Final Evaluation Report of EWP

PBGC's OIG Evaluation Report of the Early Warning Program (EWP), January 2019
Overall Conclusion - Generally the EWP is effective, but PBGC can enhance communications regarding the program.
Our Finding - We found that PBGC needs to improve communication with companies after an EWP case is opened and upon case closure.
Criteria - While EWP Case Guidance requires close out letters it did not address quality of communications and information. The GAO Federal Standards for Internal Control addresses the importance of external communication and using quality information.
Recommended Corrective Actions –   • to evaluate the effectiveness of current EWP initiation communication procedures and update as necessary to ensure companies are sufficiently informed about the program,   • implement controls to ensure close out letters are provided, and   • update their system to accurately report EWP case inventory.

Diving in further, Table 3-4 expresses the four external communication issues PBGC's OIG found regarding the EWP program.

Table 3-4. PBGC OIG's 2019 EWP External Communication Issues Findings

PBGC's OIG Findings of External Communication Issues Regarding EWP
The program could be more effective in promoting the continuation and maintenance of plans through improved **transparency** with plan sponsors and improved accountability to measure results.
We found procedures to communicate case initiation are not adequate, and **procedures to communicate** case closures have not been effective.
Some plan sponsor officials we interviewed were not aware their plan was the subject of an Early Warning Program case. (**awareness of open case**)
Some plan sponsor officials were not aware their cases were fully resolved and had been closed. (**awareness of closed case**)

The report references GAO's Standards for Internal Control in the Federal Government (2014), where <u>management</u> should **externally communicate** with the necessary **quality information** so that external parties can assist <u>management</u> in achieving the entity's objectives and address related risks.

Again, notice that it is "management" externally communicating and external parties assisting "management." However, that is not the case. In PBGC's scenario it is the Corporate Finance and Restructuring Department (CFRD) <u>analyst</u> within PBGC's Office of Negotiations and Restructuring (ONR) that is conducting the external communication; not management.

On the other hand, PBGC's CFRD's EWP Case Guidance document provides procedures for how the <u>analysts</u> are required to notify companies when cases are open (by phone) and closed (by letter). When OIG researched, the main consistent discovery finding was that the company representatives (<u>external communication</u> with plan sponsors) were not aware that their company was in the program. They also did not fully understand what being in the program and having an open case entailed. And they stated they had no prior knowledge that the program even existed.

- OIG reported: the lack of external company representative's awareness occurred because the current procedure, CFRD's EWP Case Guidance, requiring phone call notification <u>does not ensure</u> companies are sufficiently and consistently informed about the program. Current procedures increase the risk of miscommunication and program complaints. (No kidding – glad it was OIG pointing this out!)
- Further, the current phone call procedure is dependent on all analysts providing consistent information every time and is **dependent** <u>on company representatives (external people) consistently understanding this information and being able to retain and recall this information as necessary.</u>

Wait a minute. Does this mean that PBGC CFRD analyst's understanding is that the company representative, a person <u>external</u> from the organization, is *responsible* to understand the information coming *from* PBGC? Interesting. Reminder, this report began in 2018 and finalized in 2019. A cultural mindset of 2018/2019.

Aligning to the Strategic Plan

Let's now dive into PBGC's Strategic Plan for Fiscal Year 2018-2022. The first information that appears is "Message from the Director." The Director is appointed by the President and confirmed by the United States Senate. Included in the message are the following words:

> *"We actively engage with our stakeholders on the issues we face. We are <u>committed to working with our customers</u> and stakeholders <u>to find ways</u> to strengthen and sustain both the Single-Employer and Multiemployer Insurance Programs so that people can rely on them long into the future."*

In the following pages of PBGC's Strategic Plan, we next find the **core values** of the organization, as listed here:

- **Excellence is Our Commitment**. We <u>seek results</u> that embody integrity, professionalism, <u>transparency</u> and accountability.
- **Customer Service is Our Passion**. We <u>strive to provide information</u> that is timely and accurate to workers and retirees, stakeholders and partners.
- **People are Our Priority**. Our success depends on the diversity, collaboration and <u>commitment</u> of our workforce.
- **Integrity is Our Touchstone**. We perform our duties honestly, ethically and with a commitment to protecting personal privacy.
- **Innovation Guides Our Work**. We work diligently to improve our technological operations, work products and processes.

Reading just a few short words from the Director's message and the core values and now comparing them to behavioural actions that PBGC's OIG reported based on feedback they received and observed, do you feel that the analysts are "committed to working with [their] customers...to find ways" and did they "strive to provide information?"

So, while the Director and PBGC's executive management desire certain behavioural activities to occur within their organization's workforce, the reality, as pointed out by OIG's audits and evaluation, is that there is a disconnect happening.

Could the same disconnect be happening in your organization?

If there is a disconnect, that is completely okay! The first step is awareness of the disconnect. No organization is perfect. That is why there is always room for improvement. That is also why the condition for improvement will always exist.

Common Understanding

Usually within an organization as there are various activities happening, often one department doesn't communicate with the other. For example, at PBGC and according to its Customer Service Plan located within Appendix A of the Strategic Plan document, the statement reads, "[PBGC] has built a strong culture of providing services to meet the needs of its customers. PBGC considers the customer in all related activities and decisions." The marketing engagement activities are event outreach, website, newsletters, and social media.

Yet, as marketing is externally sharing the message of how customer service friendly the organization is, OIG is reporting the opposite happening within the same organization, "Despite PBGC's EWP public website, our evaluation findings—as well as information provided by the Advocate and a law firm who represents plans—suggest that there does not appear to be a common understanding of the program within the plan sponsor community. We found familiarity regarding the program lacking even among those companies who were the subject of cases. This can lead to unnecessary surprises and miscommunication. We suggest that PBGC consider additional education and outreach efforts."

This is common across many organizations. However, everyone in the organization can work together to bring awareness to prevent unnecessary surprises and miscommunication from happening. Often it becomes a finger pointing game and instead it needs to be more of an awareness game for healthy and meaningful strategy execution.

Fourth Exercise

To bring awareness in reshaping organizational structure, communication and other necessary changes, you need to align the Three E Model™ (learned in Chapter 2) with the strategic plan's goals, objectives, initiatives, and target measures.

This awareness exercise needs to happen in a bottom up and top down model. From the workforce to executive management and leadership and vice versa. Then when inconsistency or a gap is identified that is when the discovery is made. Either the change needs to happen with the Strategic Plan or with the workforce workload activities. There is always room for improvement. Everyone can help identify where that improvement needs to happen.

No matter your role in the organization, you can share your voice, contribute to the success, and make grand impacts. Everyone should be able to customize this exercise based on their daily activities and focus area. Then collaborate with their colleagues and team.

1. Take a few of your focused activities from the team's Third Exercise in Chapter 2 and insert into the appropriate Three E Model™

category. Following is a mock example using PBGC financial analyst role activities:

Internal Efficiency	Internal Effectiveness	External Effectiveness
Monitoring 1500 firms that have underfunding of $50 million or more or 5,000 participants using public sources and company reported events.	Identify transactions that are potentially of concern and engage plan sponsors for additional information.	Working with plan sponsors to obtain financial protections before a business transaction significantly increases the risk of loss

2. Looking at your Three E Model™ category, map that against your organization's current strategic plan (goals, objectives, initiatives, target measures). Following is an example set from PBGC's Strategic Plan Fiscal Year 2018-2022.

Goal #1: Preserve Plans and Protect the Pensions of Covered Workers and Retirees			
Objectives	Initiatives (Performance Strategies)	Target Measures (FY2022 Performance Goals)	Three E Model™ Category
Encourage the continuation and maintenance of pension plans	• Engage with employers, workers and pension practitioners to encourage pension plan continuation and strengthen retirement security	• Provide technical assistance and practical guidance to plan sponsors on the implementation of proposed options to reduce employer risks, while preserving plans and benefits • Prioritize simplification and transparency	(Internal Effectiveness) Identify transactions that are potentially of concern and engage plan sponsors for additional information.
	• Maintain a regulatory environment that serves stakeholders and minimizes the burdens of sponsoring a plan	• Maximize stakeholder input by holding frequent meetings and/or events with participant groups, plan sponsors, practitioner groups, industry associations, and other interested stakeholders • Perform rigorous cost-benefit analysis	

Protect workers and retirees when plans are at risk	• Preserve plans during bankruptcy and other corporate transactions	• Protect pensioners by proactively monitoring PBGC's largest exposures for transactions that may pose substantial risks to participants and retirees	**(Internal Efficiency)** Monitoring 1500 firms that have underfunding of $50 million or more or 5,000 participants using public sources and company reported events.
	• Protect the retirement security of workers and retirees and the interests of premium payers in federal courts	• Conduct a statistically significant number of audits of plans ending in standard terminations to ensure that participants receive their full retirement benefits	
		• Represent PBGC's interests in all bankruptcy cases involving defined benefit pension plans	

3. Notice what Three E Model™ category cannot be aligned against your organization's strategic plan. In the PBGC example, the External Effectiveness category could not be mapped back to the Strategic Plan. This is important to note as it is not on the executive leadership's radar of target measures for performance goals.

4. Conduct the reverse. Starting from the strategic plan, observe if any of the executive leadership's goals, objectives, initiatives, and target measures are on the radar of your team's focused activities, from Third Exercise, categorized into the Three E Model™.

Do you see how this two-way mapping activity can help an organization, like PBGC, reshape their mindsets as a collective workforce, stay organized, and communicate better by being in sync? The chances to adopt transformation, digitally and otherwise, is much greater.

When you start to align your focused activities against the organization's strategic plan, things start to shape. Regardless if it doesn't align right away, mindful communication will initiate an action to receive clarity to fill in the gaps. It is about the discovery journey through caring collaboration that matters the most during this process.

Extras

For your convenience, I have made available free downloadable Excel spreadsheet templates of the Three E Model™ to strategic plan mapping process here www.acolyst.com/communication

This is an important process, don't wait to start it.

Additionally, within the same link, I share more about organizational mission and strategic planning with examples from Chapter 1 of my first book, *The Four Intelligences of the Business Mind: How to Rewire Your Brain and Your Business for Success*.

Inspired to Reshape

Are you now inspired in reshaping mindsets to building a cohesive, collaborative, and trusting environment, no matter your role? Great!

Let's move on to the next chapter, where I explain Transformational Intelligence and how it can impact and optimize digital transformation adoption.

CHAPTER 4 – DIGITAL TALK

Digital technology allows us a much larger scope to
tell stories that were pretty much the grounds of
the literary media.
—George Lucas

TODAY'S SOCIETY is impacted by digital engagement and experience. Looking around, most corporations are focused on rebuilding themselves through digital first initiatives. But what is that? Technology, as we have continuously seen in the past decade or so, has a dramatic impact on the economy, society, and culture. Businesses are constantly looking for ways to reenergize and rewire the minds of their people and innovatively engaging the minds of their users (employees and/or clients). They are also looking for ways to be digitally disruptive; to reach, attract and connect by delivering unforeseen value. This new way of impactful thinking, to be mindful of the internal and external user application experience, is what has evolved to be known as digital transformation.

In business, two of the hardest elements to change with digital transformation initiatives are technology and culture; regardless if the end application users are employees or clients. Users, like customers, expect the web or mobile application they are using to not only have an appealing and personalized feel to it, but they also expect operations to be running smoothly and securely. The user interface design is what the user interacts, engages, and provides data to and from, thus, the application needs to be designed in such a way that is appealing, enticing, and alluring. The digital design and engagement with the data is what drives the human experience.

However, there are invisible activities happening behind the screen; servers, databases, networks, and software running constantly to give the user the experience to stay and return. This has an impact on the brand, regardless if the user is an employee, partner or a customer. Reliable habit-forming engagement to come back to and interact with.

Thus, success in the overall application is achieved when the internal organization disciplines are working in cohesive cycles with business design and technology support:

1. Designing and building brand experience using behavioral marketing techniques.

2. Ensuring the technology supporting the application experience is consistently reliable and responsive (24/7) to collect and analyze accurate and valid data being interacted to and from the user.

Differing disciplines adopting these new methodologies and approaches will include activities like human-centered design, behavior-driven development, multi-variable testing, and deep personalization to help create richer and more meaningful user experiences across the entire digital journey.

However, top technology research analyst firms, Gartner and Forrester, and analysts from the Big Three management consulting firm (McKinsey & Company, The Boston Consulting Group (BCG) and Bain & Company), constantly remind us that with digital transformation initiatives, communication issues are expected. Yet, when it comes to specifics on ways to overcome and even prevent communication matters around digital transformation projects, no one can provide a step by step action plan.

Legacy Establishments

When diving deeper, we see that the issues with adoption, organizational change and miscommunication surrounding digital transformation projects are mostly related to legacy brand establishments. The companies making waves with digital transformation, being disruptive, out beating competition, and surviving this market are those born in the digital age; the millennials. These millennial cultured organizations are delivering strong, digitally human-centric value propositions. Their generational culture is about meaning and societal purpose. If they do not feel their work has value, they will not contribute to it. That is their cultural mindset.

Can we open ourselves to learn from and understand the strengths that millennials bring with digital transformation initiatives while figuring out a way to apply them to legacy-based organizations? Yes, if we are willing!

Can mindsets shift where barriers with communication are prevented and organizational engagement are no longer struggles? Yes, if we learn how to be compassionate with ourselves and others, especially in a fast paced, results driven organization with personality dynamics!

It is important to research and define an actionable solution. Where employees and contractors of legacy organizations come together, are creative, innovative, disruptive, in a happy and engaged workplace environment. A place where they feel valued and appreciated.

Collaborating with Different Disciplines

What we know is that when dealing with digital transformation workforce, usually there are different disciplines and lines of businesses involved. Imagine the collaborative mindsets within Amazon's workforce necessary to successfully launch the free one-day delivery for Prime members. There is a need to collaborate at least two differing mindsets to make it work; the engineering, technology, logistics, science minds with the designer, artist, and visual storytelling minds. The analytical versus intuitive brain capabilities need to come together to drive human connection within the organization, from the business initiative to the user engaged experience.

There is a mindset for how to be innovative, how to gain user feedback, how to think of elevating the experience. There is a strategic mindset necessary to rethink the business. Leadership and management mindset are key to giving the "go-ahead" and moving towards a cohesive organizational culture. Inspiring workforce to rethink the way they are communicating and collaborating. The collaborative mindset could also help the different groups come to agreement on what metrics and key performance indicators (KPIs) to measure. Some thoughts for discussion could include:

- What performance targets would be reasonable and set realistic expectations of growth patterns?
- What adjustment scenarios would be needed to remain competitive, reduce cost, and provide speedy delivery?
- What are ways to add value and how do we go about it?

But how does one tap into such mindsets? Where do you start and what is the right way to launch? To change the culture within an organization for digital transformation initiatives to collaborate, communicate, connect, and coordinate with two different mindsets (analytical and intuitive), you must first understand how the brain works.

The reality is, optimizing digital transformation adoption is about reshaping the culture of the organization. It is about reshaping mindsets.

Transformational Intelligence

Certain parts of the brain are analytic, others are intuitive, other parts are social, and some are just plain anxious. The key is to realize where your own brain fits into the scheme. The rule that every individual is defined as a composite of strengths in some areas and weaknesses in others, extends to all the multifarious facets of the human brain, mind, and consciousness.

How do you base your decisions? Do you consider yourself more intuitive or analytical? If you're an intuitive decision maker, you base your decisions on "feelings" that you get. Your ideas come from bursts of creativity. If you're an analytical decision maker, you base your decisions on historical data. You crunch the numbers that your business generates and extract patterns from them. Then you use those patterns to change course as needed.

The problem is that neither of these modalities, when used separately, will transform communication within your business environment. Ideas that come from a burst of creativity, like the kind that employees spontaneously throw out in the middle of a meeting, often are not supported by data. Ideas based on data often involve doing either more, or less, of something you're already doing, rather than being based on something new.

The best way to accomplish transformation in your organization is to use an approach that combines both intuitive and analytical thinking. What I call "Transformational Intelligence."

Transformational Intelligence uses neuroscience, psychology, organizational behavior, and analytics to drive and transform business performance, while improving collaboration, communication, connection and coordination; the 4 C's.

It helps decision makers and executives drive value by providing a framework to define strategic initiatives, improve financial goals, exceed customer satisfaction, streamline business processes and tools, and motivate the workforce to make impacts; even stretching them to become innovative, creative and disruptive.

To revive the business and help connect and align the organization into rethinking and reshaping for digital transformation, a strategic look into the neuropsychology behavior approach is necessary.

Neuroscientist, Dr. Paul Zak, Director of the multidisciplinary Center for Neuroeconomics Studies (CNS) at Claremont Graduate University, believes that you can get the best results by communicating the emotional benefits of what you're trying to accomplish. "This purpose really has to be kind of what I call a core purpose, or how does your organization improve people's lives," he says. "If that's transmitted clearly and consistently, then it reinforces that we're all on the same team." Remember the story of Jeff Hoffman from Chapter 1, how he created a compassionately conscious company, Priceline.com?

Mark Waldman, Executive MBA Faculty at Loyola Marymount University, asks students enrolled in his NeuroLeadership class for 10 days, "What is your deepest innermost value?" This question causes mindset shift for what one's individual value is and can help trigger thoughts for how the individual can bring value to others and connect on a meaningful and purpose driven level.

Data Conversations

The reality is, the conversations in a business setting are not mindful of the emotional benefits for what is trying to be accomplished. The conversations are generally around the data. The flow of the data, who has access to the data, what can be done with the data, what data is missing, and much more. And the conversations about the data is generally most difficult, no matter your role in the organization: security, marketing, HR, finance, operations, sales, IT, etc.

A friend and CEO of a data governance software company shared on Twitter a snippet video of a presentation he was giving that resonates. He said, "I can't tell you how many meetings that I've been in where we argue over data. Where one person believes that this data means one thing. And another person thinks the data means another. And where does that data come from? What were the data sources? And, is it accurate data?" Yep, that is pretty much the scenario regardless of the department you are in.

Data Story

What if, just maybe, conversations about the data could be meaningful? Where the data itself does have a purpose. And the data does matter. I know you are thinking "Of course it has a purpose. Of course, data matters." What I mean is adding more life to the data. Being more mindful about it.

You see, when it comes to digital transformation strategy discussions, it starts with thinking about the data. All the pizzazz that can be done with it using digital technology. Thus, why data governance is key for digital transformation strategy initiatives. Data is generally what is used to analyze, strategize, monitor performance metrics and visualize, and make decisions via a business intelligence dashboard. But the reality is, not all business intelligence dashboard or scorecards, metrics and KPIs, and all the fancy data science analysis can give us the full story. Afterall, I led a major project with the CIO Office of the United States Postal Service on a strategy for executive data visualization for internal efficiency to communicate more effectively. Even with all the metrics, KPIs, targets, and reporting, the story to communicate the data for decision making needed to shift.

To give you a competitive edge and a deep user focus, you need to reshape how data is viewed. Why? Because not all decisions are data driven.

Amazon's Founder and Chief Executive Officer, Jeff Bezos shared in his 2018 annual letter and at the George W. Bush Presidential Center's Forum on

Leadership, that he is more interested in the story, the anecdotes, and the narrative. Amazon has a ton of metrics, but if his customers are telling him a different story than what his data is telling him, he is going to believe the customers. He explained, "The thing I have noticed is when the anecdotes and the data disagree, the anecdotes are usually right. There's something wrong with the way you are measuring it." The same goes for how meetings are conducted. They don't use PowerPoint. Instead, the focus at the beginning of the meetings are reading a six-page memo, narratively structured. Then from that, they discuss the topic in the memo. They have a conversation around it because they now have a visual story going on in their minds.

Humans can retain and recall information if it is in story format. We can bond together if the story emotionally connects.

Data-Driven Persona

Your data already has behaviors, right? You "poke" it and a "reaction" occurs. You give it "dating" rules and "protect" it. So why not also give it personality, style, character and more. Data is a living breathing subject; unless it "dies." You can also archive it to maybe "resurrect" it someday down the future.

Your data needs to have emotion. That emotional intelligence that is talked about so often and used along artificial intelligence is what will draw people to engage, if done right. Phrases such as Human-Centered, Behavioral-Centric, People-Cultured, etc., are now the trend relating to today's hot topics.

In my first book, *The Four Intelligences of the Business Mind: How to Rewire Your Brain and Your Business for Success*, in Chapter 3 titled "Customer Intelligence," I share about the personality dynamics of doing business with partners and customers. I also share about some of the process of creating customer personas for design thinking. Creating a visual storyline for what the ideal customer looks like, feels like, what their activities are and more. The same needs to be done for the journey of the data. Customer-driven personas are usually used by marketers for demand generation and campaign activities, HR for attracting talent, and app developers for user experience (UX) design.

Data-driven personas are broader and give additional creative benefits to people like strategists as they are planning, regardless of the focused division they support within the organization: marketing, HR, operations, services, etc. Why is this the case? Because of two key elements – behaviors and interests. If dealing with insurance claims, legal matters, or financial / healthcare cases, then "situations" and "circumstances" would be swapped with "interests."

However, when collaborating on the design discussion for digital technology, the **interaction dynamics** of the behaviors and interests / circumstances is what will make changes adoptable.

Referring back to Chapter 3's example of PBGC's OIG audit initiated in 2011 and finalized in 2014, OIG recommended the following:

> *"PBGC should develop a programmatic approach with consistent management and internal controls for their processes of monitoring, enforcing, and modifying negotiated funding agreements."*

The finding was:

> *"PBGC had not established a program whereby agreements are monitored, enforced and modified under uniform guidelines with adequate oversight. Because management viewed each plan sponsor individually and each agreement as unique, PBGC had not established a consistent and centrally-managed program with defined business processes and documented guidelines."*

Looking at this PBGC situation indicates that scenarios were viewed individually; case by case. The approach PBGC took was looking at it from a customer persona lens. Trying to define new business rules by applying them to the entire whole automated workflow process already in existence. However, what PBGC needed to do was reshape the way they looked at their customers, the company representatives (aka plan sponsors), and base it on select behaviors and circumstances. For starters, figuring out the many different methods customers could be grouped together based on behaviors and circumstances. Every business situation is unique, so create unique meaningful data-driven personas that work. Recognize patterns by connecting the dots.

When it comes to smart city initiatives, vendors need to rethink how to approach and operate in them. Without a connected intelligent technology infrastructure in place, streaming the data to measure ROI would be difficult. Barcelona, Spain is one of the few cities with connected intelligent infrastructure in place to record cost savings of $58 million per year on water, generated $50 million in parking revenue, and have created approximately 47,000 new jobs. Barcelona teamed with Cisco to serve its citizens and visitors. For example, Barcelona's smart bus stops are connected to the city's fiber network to display real time bus timetables. Offering USB charging sockets for smartphones and tablets, and acting as free WiFi hotspots, allows people to connect to the Internet using their mobile devices while waiting for a bus.

Mobile App Design Synergy

Referring to Chapter 1 about Chase Pay, when it comes to mobile app design, what is important for businesses to track is the interaction. Imagine the workforce team driving the technology solution. The design and product team have a thoughtful persona document put together and are sharing it with the non-design team and stakeholders. The document includes data-driven personas, anecdotes, and intuition that everyone agrees with. How does this happen?

1. They agreed from the start that all hypothetical personas are good. Everyone will have a different point of view, and that is okay. The idea is to capture as much differing views as possible, while trying to keep them to less than a 3-sentence narrative.

2. They went through existing data. They couldn't argue with what already exists. For example, PBGC could go through the feedback OIG received from plan sponsors. In your organization, you might have a customer support team or customer success group. Go through as many existing data from various sources that makes sense.

3. They recognized and accepted that design thinking is an on-going continual process that involves frequent updates as the speed of market and client demands are incessantly changing too. The trick for attracting and mesmerizing users with a positive experience is to learn from the outcome, modify processes and systems, and realign the strategy and tactics involved.

> *Note: There is a difference between "design thinking" and "user experience design" (UX Design) – some people use the terms interchangeably. Design thinking involves strategy mapping the human emotional and behavioral mindset process (effectiveness), while UX design is about enhancing the user interaction with a product via accessibility, usability, and appeal (efficiency).*

Predictive Personas

Heightening the interaction dynamics of digital design to increase technology adoption. Requires the workforce driving the solution to come up with a collaborative method to track patterns and understand predictive behaviors and unconscious habits. In addition, the workforce should have a set of questions that matters and are brought up when reflecting and prioritizing, and when engaging stakeholders during review meetings. Such example questions might be: *What connects users and keeps them engaged? What keeps them coming back for more? What drives users to make certain decisions?*

Businesses can determine predictive personas based on historical data. Prediction can be made to see what behaviors would trigger if certain events were to occur. An example would be a travel company crafting promotional incentives, real-time, based on data-driven behavioral and interest search words and patterns; learning what the buyer wants and interacting by offering customized and personalized marketing campaigns.

The data needs to have a persona characteristic, traits, and storyline. Key is starting with data that exists. Apps like Starbucks remembers existing customer's favorite drinks and is tailored to their preferences so that everyone has a unique and convenient experience. And they have it sync'd so your phone triggers a notification when you are passing by a nearby Starbucks store; indicating your custom drink can be ready by the time you walk in if you click to order via mobile device.

Masterminding Environment

To prepare the project team to rewire their minds to rethink possibilities, draw attention to new approaches, collaborate on ideas, share innovative thoughts, brainstorm, strategize, and more, the Mastermind Intelligence method should be used. It takes the basic concepts of brainstorming and makes them part of the culture of the company. The key is to create a nonjudgmental, honest, compassionate and respectful environment where everyone is inspired and committed to being creative and supportive. It is not a competition. It is an environment that is meant to feel safe and welcomed. Where no idea is a bad idea. Where even what seems like a bad idea can trigger a thought resulting to a positive breakthrough idea. It is creating an environment where everyone's attitude is striving to achieve a common goal. Then finding the best ways to make it happen.

The nonjudgmental tone of the ideation phase of Mastermind Intelligence creates an environment where all ideas are welcomed and enhances the flow of creativity. The whole point of Mastermind practices is to curiously hear all ideas, no matter how good, bad, silly, or seemingly unfeasible. Then work through them. Eliminating them one by one until the group is left with a core few with exceptional potential.

Participants need to know that there are no right or wrong answers. Conversations are only used to connect, trigger thoughts and ideas, and bring the team together to feel comfortable designing a solution for adopting digital transformational changes.

Responsibility to Communicate

The Former Deputy Under Secretary for Economic Opportunity at the U.S. Department of Veterans Affairs, Curtis Coy, shared with me a powerful quote that moved me, "How we respond to the invitation of responsibility is a personal choice!" He also shared this quote as a commencement keynote speaker for 8,000 graduating students, friends, families and faculty members at Tidewater Community College in May of 2014.

You are responsible for how you respond to the way you are invited to communicate. How you respond to the invitation of communication is a personal choice! Communication is a responsibility, regardless if you are at work or otherwise. It impacts many people and involves many factors and elements. It is your own responsibility. The communication in the workplace starts with you, no matter your role. Your individual responsibility to act.

In the following chapter, I share two more exercises that will help supercharge communication and optimize digital adoption.

Talking can transform minds, which can transform behaviours, which can transform institutions.

—SHERYL SANDBERG

CHAPTER 5 – HUMAN TRANSFORMATION

The essence of communication is intention.
—Werner Erhard

I WAS A KEY STRATEGIST for The White House, Executive Office of the President (EOP). The contract was for an enterprise digital transformation solution across all 10 agency components within EOP: The White House Office; Office of the Vice President; Office of Administration; Office of Management and Budget; Office of the United States Trade Representative; Office of National Drug Control Policy; Counsel of Economic Advisors; Counsel on Environmental Quality; National Security Council; and the Office of Science and Technology Policy.

One day, I had a meeting with the Office of the United States Trade Representative (USTR) and approximately 35 of their legal counsel who serve as the chief advisors on international trade law. USTR's mission is responsible for developing and implementing trade policies, overseeing trade negotiations with other countries, and monitoring and enforcing trade laws. USTR coordinates trade policy, resolves disagreements and frames issues for Presidential decisions.

In the room were the chief, senior, and general counsel members. I sat at the head of the room as the lawyers sat in a U-shape style setting. This was designed to help facilitate discussions. What was different with this meeting style was the lawyers did not have a table or desk in front of them, just chairs. I was the only one with a table, so I could refer to my materials and gather the information I needed.

As I observed the room, I took note of the body gestures. Knowing that some of the world's top lawyers were in that room, I knew I didn't have much time to get them to open-up and share about the project and meeting topic with their busy schedules. They were leaning back on their chairs, arms crossed, looking at each other across the room.

With my psychology background I decided to use an emotional contagion approach. Emotional contagion is when others catch, subconsciously, your mood and feel the energy of your emotion. Basically, your emotions are contagious.

That moment, I was the one responsible for setting the mood. I knew I had the power to shift things. So, what behavior did I want the legal counsel members to mimic? What did I want them to feel? What contagious emotion did I want them to "catch?"

Within myself, I needed to set the intention. My intention was to create a bond, a trusting environment, and communicate compassionately. My intent was to help and serve their needs. I was there for them.

Before the meeting began, I got up and went to individuals that were already in the room, shook their hands, introduced myself and thanked them for taking time out of their busy schedule to be there. I nicely nudged the intention of the meeting to some of them as I greeted. This tactic is slightly different than having a meeting agenda. Bringing the intention to their conscious mind prior to meeting start.

Then as the meeting began and as some late arrivers were rolling in, I sat back down, and with a smile, introduced myself, my background and my purpose for being there. I then leaned in and said, "My intention for today is to learn what matters to you and why. I am not here to talk about digital system's must-haves or desires. I truly and authentically want to know what matters to you and why." Then the body gestures started to shift. Some started to uncross their arms. Others started to sit up some.

I then said, "I know each of you have different backgrounds and experience. I genuinely want to know and learn what matters for each of you. Every single one of you have uniquely different methods to going about the way you are doing business. What I want to know is what matters to you and why." Before I could finish my sentence, a few people jumped in and began sharing, then another jumped in, and another. They shared what mattered to them and why. For example, one shared what mattered in the way he used his mobile device and why. Why that was important to him being how busy and away from his desk he was most of the time. That triggered someone else to share what mattered to them; what mattered while they were in meetings and why. And so on.

What resulted was participation. Sharing of thoughtful insight into their daily dealings. Collaborating on more effective work around ideas based on common scenarios. Cohesively evaluating what was important. And more.

And with that.... at the end, the chief counsel came up to me and said "Good meeting" with a smile. Yes, it was!

Now from a solution strategy design stand-point, I was looking for many things, like commonality, what are the "must-have" versus "nice-to-have" requirements, features and benefits, all that and many more to be later used for a requirement traceability matrix (RTM) for a digital technology implementation. But the biggest goal was driving a human-centric focused discussion. The level of inclusion, importance, and emotional connection is what drives adoption. Why? Because it becomes a shared decision-making process.

8 Steps Creating Emotional Contagion Environments

The 8 steps for creating emotional contagion environments are:

1. Set the intention. Intention of creating a meaningful bond. Feel it within yourself. Then bring it to your facial expression and your body gestures.

2. State your genuine purpose.

3. Ask "What matters to you and why?" Adding "...and why?" helps them self-reflect on why it really does matter, to them. It helps them set their own intention.

4. Create an inclusive environment. Acknowledge that everyone has a different background and experience that makes them unique and valuable. You could set a collective intention here at this step as well.

5. Express that you are there to learn from them. Learn and understand their unique situation and expectation because of it. Learn what they value.

6. Listen. Listen to help others reflect and visualize on their daily processes. Helping them express their preferences.

7. Step out of the formality. Get to know the "human-side" of things. What is really going on? What are they really dealing with? What frustrates them?

8. Have a partnership mentality. "We are in this together" attitude creates an emotional connection.

Fifth Exercise

Your turn to practice getting the best results with communication exchange, by creating an emotional contagion environment with these exercise steps:

1. Pick a topic you authentically and genuinely want feedback from your peers or teammates.

2. Request a meeting and state that you authentically and genuinely are looking for feedback on X (the subject) because of Y (how will the information you receive benefit you, the team, or the company).

3. Next state how you understand and realize everyone has a different background and experience. Also express that you do want to hear everyone's opinions toward X (the subject).

4. Lastly state, "Your feedback matters to me." You can alter the word "feedback" to what you prefer. Make sure to let them know what you are expecting from them does matter.

5. Then during the meeting go through the 8 steps for creating an emotional contagion environment.

I would be very interested to learning how this exercise went for you. Why? Because it does matter to me. What you learn and experience from this exercise can also help many others down the road. Please provide feedback and your journey by visiting www.acolyst.com/communication

Plus, in the same link, I share tips on how facial expressions and body gestures are formed via the intentions you set. Fun and informative helpful tricks I learned from a layman monk coach and some others a few years back.

Emotional Contagion in Writing

Today, most of our communication is done digitally. So, how can you create an emotional contagion environment through to the way you communicate in writing? By practicing being consciously aware of your writing style.

Here is an email communication sent to me from the president of a partner company:

Mon 4/1/2019 7:02 AM

JY

Jeremy Young <jyoung@fedresources.com>

Re: Corporate Capability Doc Updated

To   ● Valeh Nazemoff

🛈 You replied to this message on 4/1/2019 8:45 AM.

📄 Capabilities Statement One-Sheet FederalResourcesCorp - ContactJeremyYoung.pdf ▾
    620 KB

Valeh-

Thanks for sharing. Do you feel that this might be a little too large for a Corp Cap document? Have you thought about breaking out the Use Case/ Customer Successes into a separate doc?

Here is an example of the FRC Corp Cap doc....

Thoughts?

JY

Jeremy Young
President
Federal Resources Corporation
c: **301.473.3048**
o: **814.636.8025**
jyoung@fedresources.com

SEWP V: NNG15SC61B
GSA 8(a) Stars II: GS-06F-0747Z

fedresources.com

FEDERAL **RESOURCES**
CORPORATION

In response to a document I sent Jeremy via email, he responded with an emotional contagion styled approach. Now he might have done this subconsciously by practicing over the years but notice that the email contains a mix of emotional and mental stimulation. Let's break down his communication steps:

1. **Thankful.** Acknowledging receipt by thanking the person, in this case me.

2. **Do you feel.** He didn't like something based on his perception. So instead of saying what he didn't like, he asked how I felt about what he noticed. "Do you 'feel' that this might be...." – and he was right. The document I sent him was indeed too long. I am a writer after all, things do tend to get wordy with me. But of course, it was my document, so at first, I was a little hurt that my work was picked on, especially since I didn't ask for feedback. Yet, because he asked me how I "felt" I was able to pause for a moment and take another look at what he saw that maybe I didn't notice at first. Us humans can be overly sensitive sometimes (ahm... me!), and instead of responding we react based on unnecessary emotional hurt. Focus on writing to get a response, not a reaction. That was what Jeremy was aiming for and that is what he did receive in return.

3. **Consideration.** He next offered a suggestion. He didn't just leave it as he didn't like something, or was picking on my work, he followed through with a recommendation. "Have you thought about..."

4. **Visual Demonstration.** He then provided an attachment of a visual example. "Here is an example..."

5. **Feedback.** The last step was keeping me engaged and asking for my feedback on his unsolicited feedback. "Thoughts?"

Sixth Exercise

Following Jeremy's example, try the 5-step feedback approach to a solicited or unsolicited situation where you authentically and genuinely do intend to provide feedback to improve the scenario. As always, I would love to hear back from you. Please connect letting me know what changes you noticed applying this exercise by visiting www.acolyst.com/communication

Understanding our own behavior for how we communicate comes through conscious practice. Practice this writing style and the Fifth Exercise contained in this chapter. Notice: Has communication exchanges improved? What are you noticing? What are you still struggling with? Keep practicing and be patient with the results. Some seeds planted don't turn into a flower overnight.

Supercharge Communication Through Dance

Role playing emotional and behavioral exchange is best done through the practice of partnership dancing. It is a form of non-verbal communication where different dance styles can help you feel and practice the emotions within yourself that builds the external character. For example, practice getting into the character of the Samba dance creates an upbeat enthusiastic and joyful energetic emotion. When practicing and performing the Samba emotion, for example, other people in the room become contagious of your emotion and "catch" the enthusiastic and joyful energy.

Practicing dance with a partner helps mimic expressions and you will notice various facial muscles that change as well. What this creates is conscious awareness of your emotions and how your posture and facial expression aligns to it. This is great to know when to turn on and when to turn off certain emotions. Also rehearsing different styles of dance helps practice switching to different emotions within seconds. For example, when competing for Latin ballroom dancing, within seconds dancers must switch from one style to the next. They start with the Cha-Cha dance and dance for less than 2 minutes. Then there is about 10 seconds of pause before the Samba music starts where they dance for a little less than 2 minutes. Then again, another 10 seconds pause, where the same continues with the Rumba, then the Paso Doble and last the Jive. So, dancers have practiced switching characters by altering their mood through their emotions, within seconds. The key to them winning is if the judges and adjudicators can connect with their emotions and if their emotions are able to tell a story. All of this is done non-verbally.

When practicing, you and your dance partner - could be a co-worker you practice with - want to be conscious of the types of emotions you give off. Be mindful of how your emotions affects others you interact with; your partner, spectators, friends, other co-workers. Be aware of the emotion you receive from your dance partner. How are you affected by their emotion? Can you practice counter acting on their emotion to alter the mood and make changes?

Partnership dancing is one of the most effective and impactful ways to practice emotional contagion methods. Aside from the movement, learning to alter moods from dance helps shift energetic connection. I write more about this in my second book, *The Dance of the Business Mind: Strategies to Thrive Anywhere, From the Ballroom to the Boardroom.*

I want to know about your Supercharge Communication Through Dance journey. Hashtag using #SuperComDance on emotional contagion breakthroughs you experience. Power poses you come up with that alter your mood. Non-verbal dance activities that help supercharge communication. What shifts did you learn to make in your body language that you now apply at work? I want to know!

Dance the Mind, Think Your Body! Don't forget to hashtag using #SuperComDance

Encouraging and Embracing Change

You have the power to create ripple effect changes using neuro-communication techniques called "mirror neurons" or "mirroring."

Mirroring mimics facial expression, eye movements, and body language. Have you ever played with an infant where when you smiled they smiled, when you frowned they frowned, when you laughed they laughed? The child is mimicking or mirroring.

This is not the same as emotional contagion. The child that mimics the facial expression (mirroring) does not necessarily experience the same emotional state or mood (emotional contagion). However, smiling is extremely powerful in the work environment and are both mirrored and emotionally contagious; lifting moods almost immediately.

In the workplace there are other activities that can be mirrored, such as rolling the eyes that creates negative behavior. There are counter activities that can change the environment such as expressing empathy and support through nodding of the head when there is disagreement. Activities are also mirrored, such as kindness, like the First Exercise from Chapter 1. One act of kindness can mirror other acts of kindness that spread. My mother, who started the company, Acolyst, would come into work and walk around saying "Good morning!" The simple act of sharing morning cheer was mirrored and an uplift in attitude and mood would be shared. This has always been something important to her, as that would set the intention of the day for everyone at work.

Mindset perceptions can be reshaped by practicing the exercises through the chapters and applying more emotional contagion and mirroring techniques. Remember, you do have the power to supercharge workforce communication and optimize transformational success in the adoption of digital technology. I can't wait to learn more about your journey throughout the process. Make sure to connect with me and stay engaged throughout your journey!

Happy reshaping mindsets through your own conscious efforts.

WANT MORE INSIGHT?

I REALLY DO HOPE you received some "aha" moments. I live for the joy of receiving news for how my work has made a thriving impact on other people's lives. Because of this, I have more to give and want to give you more!

Fortunately, I can share more with you. Here are the action steps I need you to take to provide you more:

1.   Visit my website landing page dedicated to this book and more: http://www.acolyst.com/communication

2.   There's a section called "Want More!" – enter your information. Additionally, I would love for you to share some of the obstacles you face. Or what your mind is curious to know more about. Or what you loved and want more of. When it comes to the topic of communication, it is just too broad. Here are some of the things that might happen once you share your information and a bit more with me:

   a.   I will share with you information that I already have

   b.   I will create a response to your inquiry

   c.   I will introduce you to some of my other colleagues' work if it seems to be a better fit or the inquiry is not one of my core focus areas.

   d.   Bottom line – I will get you taken care of with more!

3. Sign up for my newsletter! This is important. Why? Because someone else might pose an awesome question or "want more of" and you will be missing out. Plus, it will keep you in the loop of some additional activities; where I will be speaking next, other people you can connect with through networking activities, case study I am working on, success impact stories, and much more. With me, there is always more!

Additional Titles by Valeh

ABOUT THE AUTHOR

Valeh Nazemoff, bestselling author of *The Four Intelligences of the Business Mind* and *The Dance of the Business Mind*, is the executive vice president and co-owner of Acolyst, a transformation strategy consulting firm.

Former Key Enterprise Solution Strategist for The White House, Executive Office of the President, Valeh's passion is in reshaping mindsets that impact transformation initiatives to drive great results. As an international public speaker and thought leader on various transformational project related subjects, including business communication, Valeh has been featured in many prestigious media publications such as Fast Company, Thomson Reuters, Wiley, SUCCESS, Entrepreneur, and Inc Magazine.

Arianna Huffington herself "loved" and invited Valeh's voice to be featured on Huffington Post, where she is now a HuffPost and Thrive Global blogger around the topics of mindful awareness and communication.

Valeh is also a regular contributor on CIO and has her own column series, "The Mindful CIO." Having a solution strategy mind with an entrepreneurial background, actively involved with analysts and university legal, business and science research, her strength includes connecting dots and recognizing patterns. Valeh enjoys problem solving and loves taking the puzzle pieces of a distressed organization then helping to create order from chaos.

Professionally known as a go-to transformational strategist and business technology expert, she has been called the "tipping point"; advising, leading and guiding complex enterprise scaled projects and teams for many government clients, including the United States Postal Services (USPS), Social Security Administration (SSA), Pension Benefit Guaranty Corporation (PBGC), and the Defense. Some of her private sector clients have included Walmart, Humana Healthcare, JP Morgan Chase, FedEx, and Toyota.

Known as a firefighter with 15+ years' experience, Valeh brings her energy and intention to helping businesses stay on track with its mission, initiatives and strategy. With her psychology background in organizational behavior and the inclusion of neuroscience research in her works for dynamics, communication, collaboration, engagement and emotional intelligence, she leads by helping organizations reimagine the cultural value and benefits for mindset shifts.

Valeh is the recipient of several leadership awards and was recognized for seven consecutive years on CRN Magazine's Women of the Channel lists. She has coached and conducted workshops with attendees from Harvard University, IBM, and Erie Insurance. She has taught and mentored students from George Mason University, University of Mary Washington, University of Phoenix, and Marymount University on various business topics and skills. Valeh has a BS in psychology with a focus on organizational behavior and two MBAs; one in e-business and the other global management.

Most of all, she loves to partner dance the Rumba, Cha Cha, Samba, Paso Doble and the Argentine Tango. She invites comments and inquires at valeh.nazemoff@acolyst.com. So, if you need a super woman who can roll up her sleeves, put out fires and get the entire organization aligned, then you need to contact her now. She just might share how she magically waves her wand to solve what seems to you as problems, but to her something that just needs a sparkly flair (after putting on her dancing shoes, of course!)

For more information about the author, visit her websites at www.acolyst.com and www.valehnazemoff.com

AUTHOR ENGAGEMENT

Project Related Engagements:

Studies and research point out that about 90% of transformational project issues are communication related. As Acolyst's executive vice president and co-owner, Valeh is excited to help you get ahead of those foreseen issues and assist in mitigating out of it if you are currently having them. With focus on *Workforce of the Future* and *Digital Transformation* initiatives there are lots of multi-generational and multi-cultural dynamics that occur with inclusive behavioral issues needing to overcome.

Valeh has created neuropsychology behavioral strategy solutions for large enterprise complex organizations focusing on various initiatives such as data visualization, advanced analytics, BI, digital transformation, cognitive computing (ai), machine learning, deep learning, robotic process automation and governance. Initiatives involving user experience (employee, customer and partner) needs a human-centric approach. Human-centric approach involves mindful collaboration, cohesiveness, connection, and communication. Valeh knows how to supercharge the workforce to communicate so the organization can excel and thrive on remaining focused on the executive strategy plan while aligning with leader driven cross-departmental activities.

For an assessment, strategy plan and beyond, contact her at valeh.nazemoff@acolyst.com

acolyst

Transforming Business Performance

Speaking, Coaching, Retreats & Other Engagements:

For several years now, Valeh has crafted and refined a unique communication transformation business workshop that will reshape your mindset. Her system helps participants gain clarity and connect to the rhythm of communication. More about her workshop can be found by visiting the link here: http://www.acolyst.com/communicationworkshop

Customized programs can also be arranged for international speaking engagements, private mentoring, group coaching, half-day, full-day or multi-day workshops, sponsored dinner forums and even delightful getaway retreats (which enhances the experience as she adds additional special highlighted memorable elements). Retreats can be private, or group based.

And certainly, if you have a creative vision of an engagement in your mind, do reach out and connect. Further, Valeh is connected to other leading experts in other focus areas. If it is a topic that requires co-collaboration efforts to help you and your group reach your highest potential, have a talk, as innovative creations are her forte. Valeh will inspire and energize through her passionate and engaging style. You'll be entertained, motivated and enlightened.

Contact today to discuss a plan to be added to her schedule. Reach the team at contact@acolyst.com or her directly at valeh.nazemoff@acolyst.com

Connect with her via social media:
LinkedIn: https://www.linkedin.com/in/valehnazemoff/
Twitter: https://twitter.com/valehnazemoff
Facebook: https://www.facebook.com/OfficialValehNazemoff/
Instagram: https://www.instagram.com/valehnazemoff/

ACKNOWLEDGEMENTS

I N LIFE YOU ARE FACED WITH DECISIONS. Sometimes you act on them, other times you don't. For those you act on, some turn out good and others not so much. When you take courageous risks, sometimes you succeed and other times you fail. What matters is who is there, lifting you up and lifting you higher. Who enthusiastically, with a pure heart, can't wait to hear what adventure you are up to next. And only questions how they can support you on your effort, even if they are in the background, simply there just to cheer you on. What matters is the person who changes 3 planes and drives 3 hours more to hear you speak because you matter. What matters is who you get to share the journey of your story with. Jeremy Young, thank you for making me feel I matter. Thank you for jumping in and supporting me on this project. Thank you for the optimism you always bring, no matter how crazy and far off my ideas are. And thank you for being amazingly you. I am forever grateful for your compassionate friendship and mostly for believing and trusting in me, always. With loving gratitude!

Thank you to my collaboration team. I am very fortunate and incredibly lucky for all the magical miracles you, my angles, bring.

My clients, past and present, who inspire me to write the stories. I continue to learn and grow so much! Appreciate experiencing this journey.

Finally, my mother who has been my lifelong teacher, my strength, and endless supporter – thank you for your unconditional love! Love you!

I'd say the key to a good relationship is communication.

—MANDY MOORE

REFERENCES

Amazon.com, Inc. Company News. "Amazon's 2018 Letter to Shareholders." amazon.com. April 11, 2019. https://blog.aboutamazon.com/company-news/2018-letter-to-shareholders

JPMorgan Chase & Co. Investor Relations. "JPMorgan Chase Strategic Update." jpmorganchase.com. February 27, 2018. https://www.jpmorganchase.com/corporate/investor-relations/document/3cea4108_strategic_update.pdf

Pension Benefit Guaranty Corporation (PBGC) "Strategic Plan: FY 2018-2022." pbgc.gov. March 30, 2019. https://www.pbgc.gov/sites/default/files/pbgc-strategic-plan-2018-2022.pdf

Pension Benefit Guaranty Corporation (PBGC) Office of Inspector General (OIG). "Audit Report: Increased Oversight, Internal Controls and Performance Accountability Needed for PBGC's Monitoring, Enforcing and Modifying Negotiated Funding Agreements." oig.pbgc.gov. March 21, 2014. https://oig.pbgc.gov/pdfs/PA-11-80.pdf

United States General Accounting Office (GAO). "Human Capital: Key Principles for Effective Strategic Workforce Planning." gao.com. December 11, 2003. https://www.gao.gov/assets/250/240816.pdf

United States General Accounting Office (GAO). "Standards for Internal Control in the Federal Government." gao.com. September 10, 2014. https://www.gao.gov/assets/670/665712.pdf

YOUR NOTES

To effectively communicate, we must realize that we are all different in the way we perceive the world and use this understanding as a guide to our communication with others.

—TONY ROBBINS

The most important thing in communication is hearing what isn't said.

—PETER DRUCKER

Humor is the affectionate communication of insight.

—LEO ROSTEN

Dance is communication, and so the great challenge is to speak clearly, beautifully and with inevitability.

—MARTHA GRAHAM

Dance is about movement and can be an art, but it's also about communication – with yourself, as much as with other people.

—JAN MURRAY

Communication works for those that work at it.

—JOHN POWELL

Emotional awareness is necessary so you can properly convey your thoughts and feelings to the other person.

—JASON GOLDBERG

Good communication is as stimulating as coffee, and just as hard to sleep after.

—ANNE MORROW LINDBERGH

Be sincere; be brief; be seated.

—FRANKLIN D. ROOSEVELT

Communication is power. Those who have mastered its effective use can change their own experience of the world and the world's experience of them. All behavior and feelings find their original roots in some form of communication.

—TONY ROBBINS

In many ways, effective communication begins with mutual respect, communication that inspires, encourages others to do their best.

—ZIG ZIGLAR

Photography, as a powerful medium of expression and communications, offers an infinite variety of perception, interpretation and execution.

—ANSEL ADAMS

Communication is the essential medium of a creative culture: the communal sea in which we all swim. A company that can't communicate is like a jazz band without instruments: Music just isn't going to happen.

—JOHN KAO

Animal language is a contagious expression of mood effecting communication between social partners.

—ROBERT ARDREY

♪

Nonverbal communication is an elaborate secret code that is written nowhere, known by none, and understood by all.

—EDWARD SAPIR

Communication is a science as well as an art. What does speaking precisely mean? You are consciously communicating with another person at that person's frequency, not yours.

—HARBHAJAN SINGH YOGI

*The single biggest problem in communication
is the illusion that it has taken place.*

— GEORGE BERNARD SHAW

VALEH NAZEMOFF

VALEH NAZEMOFF

VALEH NAZEMOFF

VALEH NAZEMOFF